EXTINCT SPECIES

EXTINCT MAMMALS

First published in 2002 by
Grolier Educational
Sherman Turnpike
Danbury, Connecticut 06816
© Quartz Editions 2002

Library of Congress Cataloging-in-Publication Data
Extinct species.
    p. cm.
  Contents: v. 1. Why extinction occurs - - v. 2. Prehistoric animal life - - v. 3. Fossil hunting - - v. 4. Extinct mammals - - v. 5. Extinct birds - - v. 6 Extinct underwater life - - v. 7. Extinct reptiles and amphibians - - v. 8. Extinct invertebrates and plants - - v. 9. Hominids - - v. 10. Atlas of extinction.
  Summary: Examines extinct species, including prehistoric man, and discusses why extinction happens, as well as how information is gathered on species that existed before humans evolved.
ISBN 0-7172-5564-6 (set) - - ISBN 0-7172-5565-4 (v. 1) - - ISBN 0-7172-5566-2 (v. 2) - - ISBN 0-7172-5567-0 (v. 3) - - ISBN 0-7172-5568-9 (v. 4) - - ISBN 0-7172-5569-7 (v. 5) - - ISBN 0-7172-5570-0 (v. 6) - - ISBN 0-7172-5571-9 (v. 7) - - ISBN 0-7172-5572-7 (v. 8) - - ISBN 0-7172-5573-5 (v. 9) - - ISBN 0-7172-5574-3 (v. 10)
  1. Extinction (Biology) - - Juvenile literature. 2. Extinct animals - - Juvenile literature. [1. Extinction (Biology) 2. Extinct animals.] I. Grolier Educational.

  QH78 .E88 2002
  578.68 - - dc21   2001055702

Produced by Quartz Editions
Premier House
112 Station Road
Edgware HA8 7BJ
UK

EDITORIAL DIRECTOR: Tamara Green
CREATIVE DIRECTOR: Marilyn Franks
PRINCIPAL ILLUSTRATOR: Neil Lloyd
CONTRIBUTING ILLUSTRATORS: Tony Gibbons, Helen Jones
EDITORIAL CONTRIBUTOR: Graham Coleman

Reprographics by Mullis Morgan, London
Printed in Belgium by Proost

ACKNOWLEDGMENTS

The publishers wish to thank the following for supplying photographic images for this volume.

Front & back cover t SPL/J.Baum & D.Angus

Page 1t SPL/J.Baum & D.Angus;
p3t SPL/J.Baum & D.Angus; p11c BAL;
p12tr OSF/B.Gibbons; p13tc NHPA/B.Gibbons;
p17t SPL; p17bc NHPA/K.Schafer;
p19tc NHPA/D.Heuclin; p19bl NHM/M.Long;
p21b NHPA/W.Paton; p29br OSF/S.Meyers/Okapia;
p31tl OSF/B.Bennett; p33tc OSF/K.Atkinson;
p34cl NHPA/D.Watts; p34bl NHPA/D.Watts;
p36tr OSF/N.Benvie; p39tl OSF/T.Ulrich;
p41tl Port Lympne Zoo; p43tl NHPA/D.Watts;
p45br OSF/B.Bennett.

Abbreviations: Bridgeman Art Library (BAL); Natural History Museum (NHM); Natural History Photographic Agency (NHPA); Oxford Scientific Films (OSF); Science Photo Library (SPL); bottom (b); center (c); left (l); right (r); top (t).

EXTINCT SPECIES

EXTINCT MAMMALS

GROLIER EDUCATIONAL

SHERMAN TURNPIKE, DANBURY, CONNECTICUT 06816

STRIPED LIKE A TIGER
More like a wolf, except for its stripes, this last thylacine, or Tasmanian tiger, died in 1936, as described on pages 34-35.

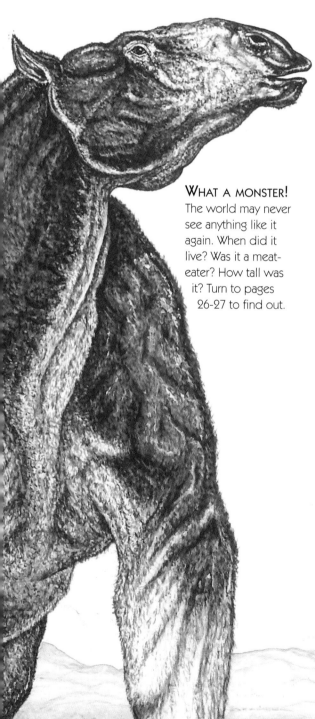

WHAT A MONSTER!
The world may never see anything like it again. When did it live? Was it a meat-eater? How tall was it? Turn to pages 26-27 to find out.

Contents

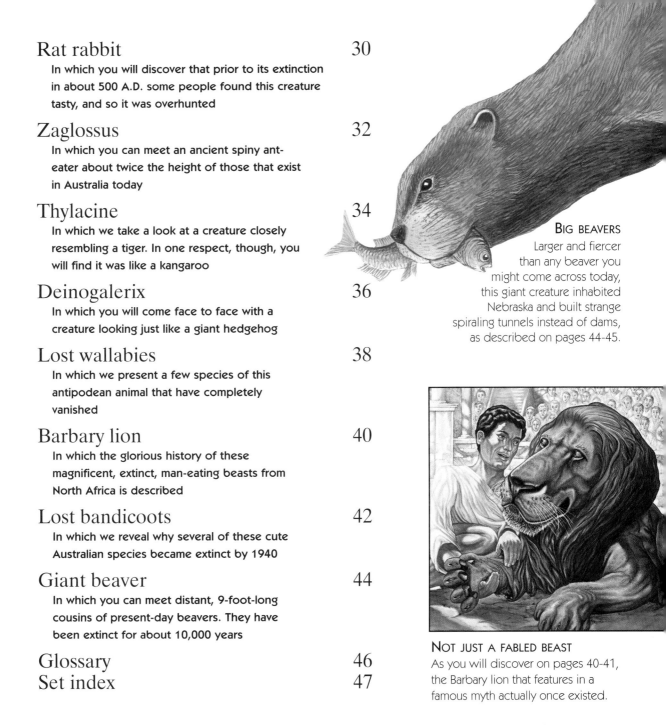

BIG BEAVERS
Larger and fiercer than any beaver you might come across today, this giant creature inhabited Nebraska and built strange spiraling tunnels instead of dams, as described on pages 44-45.

NOT JUST A FABLED BEAST
As you will discover on pages 40-41, the Barbary lion that features in a famous myth actually once existed.

FOUND AS A FOSSIL
To discover its name, habitat, and the era when this extraordinary creature lived, turn to pages 36-37.

INTRODUCTION

As you turn the pages that follow, you will find yourself embarking on a very unusual sort of safari. What makes this journey so special is the fact that not one of the mammals – creatures that give birth to live young and suckle them – you will meet still exists.

Some of the creatures featured were last seen hundreds of thousands of years ago – the extraordinary *Chalicotherium*, for example. It looked like a cross between a ground sloth, a gorilla, and a horse!

But there have been far more recent disappearances. A primate known as Miss Waldron's red colobus monkey, once common in Ghana and elsewhere in that region of West Africa, for instance, became extinct as recently as the year 2000.

The reasons why such mammals have vanished are many and varied, as you are about to discover.

DELIGHTFULLY DINKY
This extinct miniature elephant, which was once only found on the Mediterranean island of Sicily, was a lot smaller than you.

WILD SPECIMEN
The fastest and boldest of asses, the Syrian species, finally died out in 1928. Human greed had a lot to do with this.

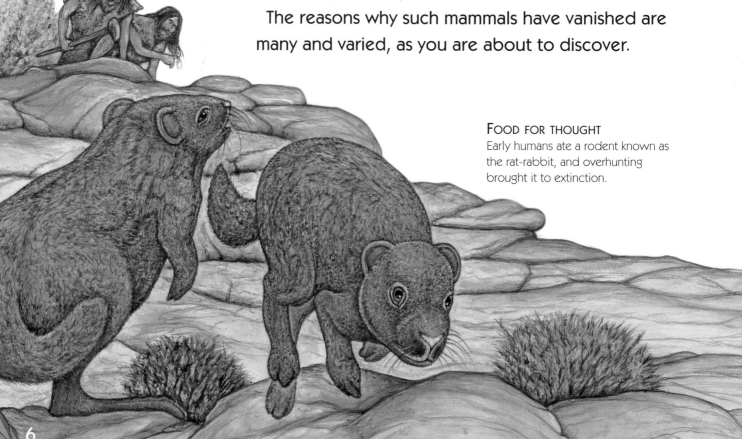

FOOD FOR THOUGHT
Early humans ate a rodent known as the rat-rabbit, and overhunting brought it to extinction.

In some cases they could not adapt to changes in climate. Their natural habitat may have been destroyed either due to environmental disaster or through human intervention. In other instances they were hunted excessively by humans either for food or for sport.

We invite you now to come face to face with such fascinating beasts as the lost tarpans of eastern Europe, the quaggas of southern Africa, and the giant beavers of North America. They are all sadly lamented. Just occasionally, however, there is a glimmer of hope that creatures once thought extinct may yet be sighted in very remote areas, as optimistic natural history experts think may well be the case with the kouprey.

Conservationists are certainly to be supported in their sterling efforts to get us to take greater care in future of Earth's surviving mammals, and a good place to begin is with an appreciation of some of them that, alas, are no more.

A FEARSOME FOX
Many shipwrecked sailors are known to have been attacked by packs of the aggressive creatures, *above*, once found only on the Falkland Islands.

SPIRITED BEASTS
Extinct since the late 19th century, tarpans, like those shown *right,* once roamed the plains of eastern Europe and western Asia. But why did these magnificent wild horses, the subject of a fascinating Mongolian legend, die out?

THE QUAGGA

Since 1878 the world has mourned the very last quagga (<u>KWAG</u>-AH) to be killed in the wild. The grasslands of Africa may never see their like again, for although a zoo once had a specimen, it died without breeding.

Early Dutch settlers reaching the part of Africa where the quagga lived first called this animal the *quahah kwah-hah* in imitation of the noise it made. Only later was the name shortened to its present form.

If you looked at the quagga from the front, you might easily have mistaken it for a zebra. After all, it was the right shape and seemed to have a striped body. But a little way down its back the stripes suddenly faded to an all-over color. From the rear it was more like a mule.

The quagga's mane was tidy and short, running the length of its neck, and at the top of its head there were short tufts of hair, too.

Toward the end of its thin tail the quagga also had a thick cluster of dark hairs, useful for flicking away flies in the tropical heat.

ON GUARD

Early settlers needed to protect their livestock since there was always risk of attack by wild creatures such as jackals. Many farmers therefore worked hard at training quaggas to act much like guard dogs. This was so successful that these creatures even learned to call out loudly at any sign of the approach of a likely predator.

THE AFRICAN VELD
The natural habitat of the quagga was the area around the Cape of Good Hope in southern Africa. Here the open grasslands, or veld, provided an ideal environment for this plant-eater. The climate was warm, and there was ample rainfall to ensure good grazing grounds.

In their natural environment quaggas lived in groups in order to protect their young. Like the zebra, the quagga was a plant-eater, grazing mainly on grass. It lived peacefully alongside ostriches and wildebeests, a "cooperative" that had distinct advantages.

Wildebeests have a keen sense of smell, and ostriches have good eyesight as well as being constantly on the alert.

HOW THE QUAGGA WAS LOST
At the beginning of the 19th century huge herds of quaggas roamed the veld, but settlers hunted them mercilessly. They used their meat for food and also prized their skins for making bags and other goods.

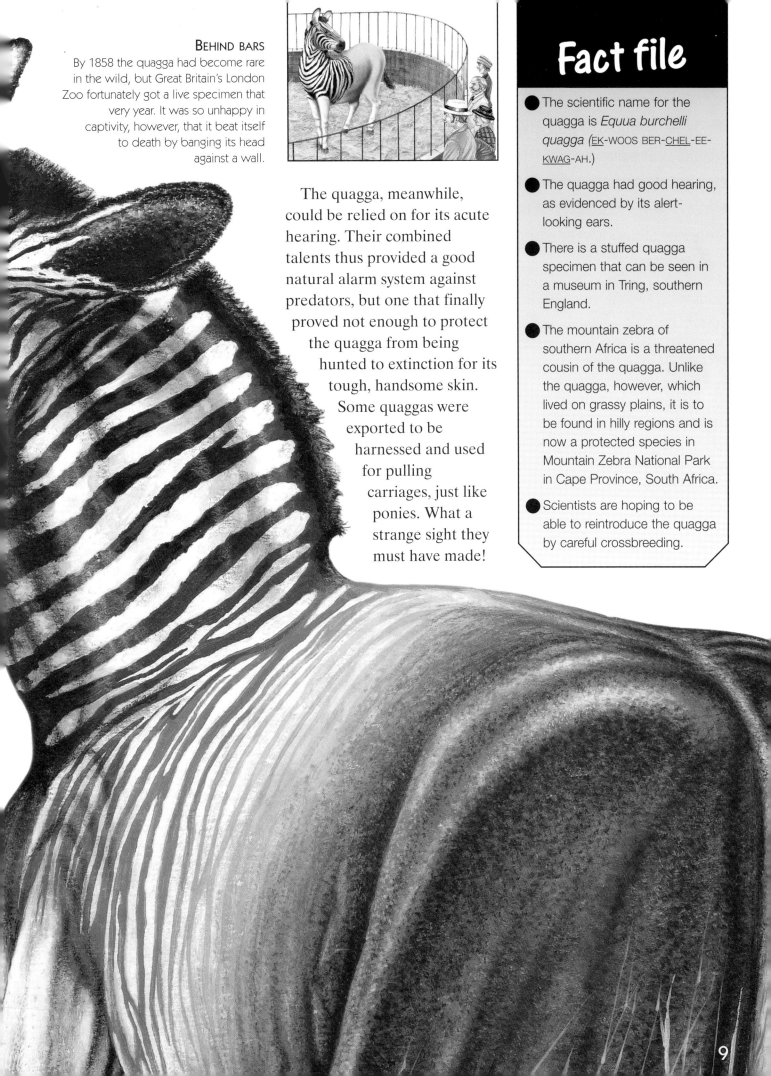

BEHIND BARS
By 1858 the quagga had become rare in the wild, but Great Britain's London Zoo fortunately got a live specimen that very year. It was so unhappy in captivity, however, that it beat itself to death by banging its head against a wall.

The quagga, meanwhile, could be relied on for its acute hearing. Their combined talents thus provided a good natural alarm system against predators, but one that finally proved not enough to protect the quagga from being hunted to extinction for its tough, handsome skin. Some quaggas were exported to be harnessed and used for pulling carriages, just like ponies. What a strange sight they must have made!

Fact file

- The scientific name for the quagga is *Equua burchelli quagga* (EK-WOOS BER-CHEL-EE-KWAG-AH.)

- The quagga had good hearing, as evidenced by its alert-looking ears.

- There is a stuffed quagga specimen that can be seen in a museum in Tring, southern England.

- The mountain zebra of southern Africa is a threatened cousin of the quagga. Unlike the quagga, however, which lived on grassy plains, it is to be found in hilly regions and is now a protected species in Mountain Zebra National Park in Cape Province, South Africa.

- Scientists are hoping to be able to reintroduce the quagga by careful crossbreeding.

DWARF ELEPHANTS

We usually think of elephants as large and bulky. So would you believe that there were once dwarf elephants that stood only about three feet tall as adults? Their fossils have mainly been found on the island of Sicily. Just imagine how tiny their babies were!

Why is it that such a tiny species of elephant evolved when, elsewhere, elephants remain among the largest creatures we know today? Paleontologists have come up with a fascinating explanation to show why miniature species, such as the dwarf elephants, are sometimes found only in an island environment.

When they reached the island of Sicily from Africa and established a new habitat there, elephants would have found limited resources. There were also probably no giant predators. So the immigrant elephants did not need to maintain their original body size and became smaller over time. It may even be that the existence of lightweight dwarf elephants lies behind accounts of the giant rokh, or so-called elephant bird, which is said to have been able to lift up an elephant – or, more likely, a dwarf elephant – into the air, then dropping it to its death.

PINT-SIZED
The dwarf elephant, shown *left*, was smaller when mature than a baby African elephant is today.

10

Some experts even believe that the origin of the famous Greek myth about the one-eyed cyclops, Polyphemus, in Homer's epic The Odyssey arose due to the early discovery of fossils of dwarf elephants. Indeed, these fossilized skeletal remains could well have led to a major misunderstanding. There was a large central hole in the skull, which might have been thought to be the site of the huge central eye that the fantasy creature, the cyclops, was described as having.

LOST AND FOUND

The dwarf elephants of Sicily have long disappeared. In Africa, meanwhile, a type of pygmy elephant, not as tiny as the dwarf elephants of Sicily but still considerably smaller than any other known elephant, has sometimes been reported. Bad-tempered and reddish in color, it is said to have a tropical forest habitat in Zaire, Gabon, Liberia, and the Central African Republic.

One young male specimen, under 4 feet high, was captured about 100 years ago and, after careful study, declared a new subspecies of the African elephant. It was taken to the Bronx Zoo, New York, where it grew three more feet. Even then, it was smaller than the average mature elephant we know today.

However, what was strange about this specimen, named Congo by his keepers, was that its tusks were almost two feet long and so entirely out of proportion with its body.

Some zoologists concluded that it may merely have been a stunted or juvenile specimen of a more familiar type of elephant. But when a female pygmy elephant was captured, it was found to be pregnant and so would have been an adult. The pygmy elephant has also been spotted in herds of only its own kind. A number of scientists therefore contend it is an entirely separate species.

BELIEVE IT OR NOT
The 13th-century traveler Marco Polo, *right*, was astonished to learn of a bird so huge that it was capable of lifting up an elephant, though probably the dwarf species.

LOST GOATS

People taking a vacation on the Mediterranean island of Majorca are often surprised to find the fossils of tiny prehistoric goats displayed as museum exhibits there.

ROCKY HABITAT
The photograph *above* shows the sort of environment in which the tiny goats of the island of Majorca would have lived when venturing out of their cave homes.

As far as paleontologists know, cave goats did not live anywhere other than Majorca, an island off the coast of Spain. They were tiny in comparison with the type of goats with which we are familiar today. In fact, a cave goat was only about 20 inches tall when fully grown. However, it is often the case that animals living on islands evolve to become smaller than normal if there are no dangerous predators sharing their habitat.

JUST LIKE KIDS
Even when mature, prehistoric cave goats, like those in this illustration, were only the size of newborn kids today.

LIVING TOGETHER

Cave goat skulls have been found with filed horns, providing an almost certain indication that they would have been kept as domesticated animals by the early humans with whom they are likely to have shared cave dwellings.

Indeed, in one particular deep-lying cave the remains of several hundred of these diminutive extinct goats were found alongside shards of primitive pottery and the bones of early settlers. It seems that about 6,000 years ago, humans and goats alike must have fallen by accident into a crevice that led down to this cave.

Apart from an occurrence like this, early humans may well have chosen to live alongside these goats. Since the creatures were so small, they would not have taken up much room in the shared caves. What was more, early humans would have found it very convenient to feed on their meat since it would have meant they did not need to go hunting so often when the weather was bad. They may also have obtained nourishment by milking the adult females.

MINIATURE MOTHER AND CHILD
An adult prehistoric cave goat was as small as the 21st-century baby goat, shown *above* with its mother. So imagine how tiny a newborn cave goat was!

Proof that these tiny goats shared living quarters with human cave-dwellers comes not only from the finding of their bones but their coprolites. Some caves also contain wall paintings of the goats.

Most paleontologists doubt, however, that the cave goat spent much time in the caves in spite of its common name. It must have ventured out to look for food and probably mostly munched on woody bark, using its enlarged lower incisor teeth, which grew constantly, to strip it off. The cave goat would also have grazed on whatever grass or shrubs it could find.

Fact file

- Remains of the Majorcan cave goat were first found on the island in 1968.

- In spite of their name, cave goats also spent time outdoors.

- The large lower incisor teeth of a prehistoric cave goat were much like those of a beaver.

- Cave goats were good climbers and would have been able to cope very easily with the steep slopes in some parts of Majorca.

- The tiny cave coat would not have weighed more than a few pounds at the most, even as an adult.

- The horns of cave goats were once used on the island of Majorca as talismans or lucky charms.

RECENT EXTINCTION

In January 2000 another type of goat was declared extinct. It lived in northern Spain but went into decline due to environmental changes and the effects of poaching. The last living specimen was a 13-year-old female found crushed under a tree.

LOST BEARS

Most large bears are undoubtedly dangerous if approached and so have often been hunted. But now a number of species have completely disappeared in the wild for other reasons, too.

MISSING IN MEXICO

By 1960 only 30 Mexican grizzlies were known to exist. But they soon disappeared, too, due to poisoning, hunting, and trapping.

The Atlas bear of North Africa, where lots of its fossilized remains have been found, is lost forever but did not finally become extinct until the end of the 19th century.

Back in Roman times many were taken for display in the arena. Then later, when firearms became generally available, a great number were shot not only because they were potential attackers but because their pelts were considered valuable. Their gradual demise is also likely to have been due to deforestation.

LOST HABITAT

Killed for sport since ancient times, the Atlas bear finally became extinct due to destruction of its North African forest environment.

The American continent has also lost a bear – the Mexican grizzly, which was among its largest indigenous animals. At one time this bear's habitat was extremely widespread, stretching from northern regions down to Arizona, Kansas, and Texas, then on to southern California and New Mexico, and finally to Mexico itself.

A magnificent creature, it measured approximately 6 feet in length and weighed about 750 pounds – as much as four adult men. Finally, it was declared extinct in 1964.

IN DANGER TODAY

Hunting and loss of natural habitat are also principal causes of the severe decline of the spectacled bear of South America. Fewer than 2,000 are now thought to exist. Their natural habitat is the cloud forest of Peru, Bolivia, Ecuador, Colombia, and Venezuela; but much of this secluded environment has been destroyed over recent years in favor of land to be used for subsistence farming.

A very attractive bear, with white markings encircling its eyes – hence its name – it is also hunted by the local population, some of whom believe its organs can be used as forms of medicine, though there is no proof that they are effective as cures for any conditions or diseases.

The polar bear, which lives in Arctic regions, is also severely endangered partly due to hunting, mostly from the air, but also because of global warming and the effect on its food supplies.

In the very north of Canada, for example, in the year 2000 ice started to melt three weeks earlier in the spring than it once did, which gave the bears a shorter time to hunt for seals – their staple diet. Polar bears are excellent swimmers but prefer to catch their prey from an ice platform. Fortunately, countries such as Norway, Denmark, Siberia, Canada, and the U.S. are now doing all they can to protect the polar bears' Arctic environment.

IN PERIL
A polar bear's hide fetches a very high price, and so its numbers are rapidly declining. Pollutants and global warming are also to blame.

FALKLANDS FOX

Strangely, at one time some Falkland Islanders who shared this creature's habitat believed it was a vampire of some kind, perhaps because they saw it dripping with blood after a kill. But that is just one of several reasons why it had been hunted to extinction by 1876.

The newsletter of a Falklands conservation society has been named *The Warrah* after an alternative name for the lost Falklands fox, the only mammal, apart from mice, known to have been endemic to this group of islands lying off the coast of Argentina.

This fox (sometimes also called the Antarctic wolf, though the term fox is more usual) was in fact long persecuted on the Falkland Islands. Here they were once regularly killed after being lured with a piece of meat and then stabbed to death.

Back in 1764 a few sailors were attacked by some Falklands foxes, probably because the animals were terrified by these mariners. As a result, the men deliberately set an extensive area of grass on fire to try and drive the foxes from one particular island.

The blaze is said to have lasted for several days, and no doubt many of the foxes did not survive the terrible inferno.

The 19th-century naturalist Charles Darwin saw the Falklands fox for himself when he sailed to this part of the world, and he predicted it would become extinct before too long.

TAME EXCUSE

The Falklands fox and its cubs are said to have been friendly by nature, which may be why they were easily shot and speedily became extinct.

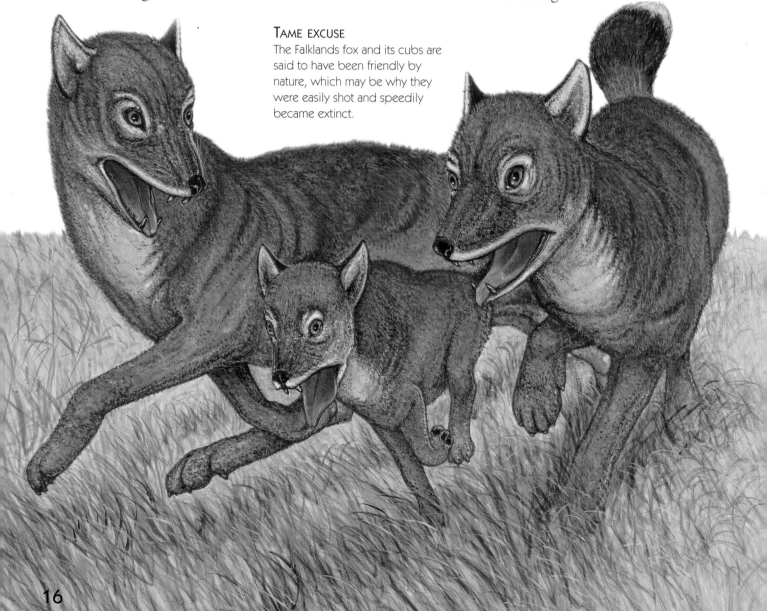

16

BRILLIANT PROPHECY
When the 19th-century naturalist Charles Darwin sailed on his ship the *Beagle*, shown *above*, to study wildlife and find new specimens, he came across the Falklands fox but foresaw that it would die out altogether as the islands' human population increased.

Indeed, in his book *Zoology of the Voyage of the Beagle* Darwin wrote that:

"The number of these animals during the past fifty years must have been greatly reduced; already they are entirely banished from that half of East Falkland which lies east of the head of San Salvador Bay and Berkeley Sound; and it cannot, I think, be doubted that as these islands are now being colonized, before the paper is decayed on which this animal has been figured, it will be ranked among those species which have perished from the earth."

The Falklands fox was hunted for its pelt, which was turned into fur coats. It was also said by farmers on the islands to kill lots of sheep and so was shot whenever possible to keep its numbers down.

Most mysterious, however, was the fact that it was the only large mammal or predator on the islands apart from the human population. So how did it manage to find sufficient food? It is no wonder it preyed on sheep. When it could not catch one, we can only assume it must have lived on penguin meat, eggs, and perhaps vegetation. There was certainly a shortage of food for it, and one report says that it was common for the Falklands fox to live off its own stored body fat for part of the year.

REMOTE ISLAND HABITAT
Wildlife experts remain baffled as to how the Falklands fox could have been the only four-legged animal in this remote region apart from mice.

BODY TALK

What, then, were the main physical characteristics of this fox? It was about 4-5 feet long but just 2 feet tall. Its underparts were white, unlike its thick coat, which was a blend of brown, black, and yellow; and its tail, tipped with a white border, was full, too.

The warrah had a pointed, black-tipped snout and alert-looking ears. Its teeth were those of a typical carnivore, and the upper jaw extended further forward than the bottom one. But although this description sounds like that of a wolf or fox, it was not in fact related to them, and scientists are still perplexed by its origins.

AUROCHS

The last aurochs (<u>OW</u>-ROKS) died in an eastern European forest in 1630. For some time Polish rulers had been aware of the need to protect this species which had vanished completely from other parts of the continent. But why did it survive for so long in Poland?

SOLID EVIDENCE
Prehistoric cave paintings, like the one shown here, together with fossilized remains, have provided paleontologists with accurate renderings of the main physical features

A primitive type of wild ox, this creature was about 6.5 feet in height and had very long horns that often extended to nearly 3 feet in length. It was a direct ancestor of the domestic cattle known in Europe today and of the black fighting bulls of Spain. In prehistoric times the aurochs inhabited most of Europe and Asia, and was extensively hunted by humans.

Paleontologists think that the aurochs probably survived far longer in Poland than anywhere else in Europe because of medieval royal protection and laws against hunting. Only when forests were cleared for new settlements did many different species of animals go into decline.

SEEN BY CAESAR

But the aurochs had been admired since ancient times. Indeed, the great Roman Emperor Julius Caesar described them as follows in his work *De Bello Gallico* (a Latin title which, in translation, means *About the Gallic War*):

"They are only a little smaller than elephants and are related to bulls. They are very strong and can run very fast.

MAKING A MODERN EQUIVALENT
Through careful selective breeding a creature closely resembling the extinct aurochs has been produced, as shown in the photograph *above*.

"No one is safe when they are around. They cannot be tamed, even when they are young. Anyone who kills a great number proudly displays their horns as proof of this achievement and is greatly honored.

"The horns differ from those of our oxen and are widely sought after. Edged with silver, they make excellent drinking vessels which are used at important feasts."

But it was not only in Roman times that the aurochs was sought after. From the 16th-century writings of Conrad Gessner we can gather they were hunted with extreme cruelty in lands outside Polish jurisdiction.

Fact file

- The aurochs survived for longest in Poland. This was mainly because it could only be hunted by the Polish monarch in medieval times; and the rulers did this in moderation. There are even examples of royal relatives being refused permission to slay an aurochs by the king.

- Special men were employed to protect the aurochs and to feed them in winter. In return, these farmers paid no taxes.

- Some aurochs are known to have perished due to diseases caught from other types of cattle.

- When one of the last aurochs died, its horns were set in metal and sent to the Polish king. They are now in the royal armory in Stockholm, Sweden.

It seems that other European royalty welcomed the presentation of aurochs meat. In Gessner's own words:

"One individual aurochs is made to separate from the rest of the herd and is then hunted by many men and dogs, often for a long while. The aurochs only falls when it is hit in the chest. While it is still alive, the skin between its horns will then be ripped off. This is sent, with the heart and its fresh, salted meat to the king."

WILD ANCESTORS
The models shown *left* are restorations of the wild prehistoric aurochs, an ancestor of our present day domestic cattle.

Lost Horses

Early horses were small; but as some species disappeared, others taking their place over many millions of years became larger and faster. Why did such changes occur? And are some types of horse existing today in danger of disappearing altogether?

Prehistoric horses lived in forested regions, and it was advantageous to remain small in this sort of habitat. But once they moved to open plains where they could run freely, their limbs became longer. Their skulls and teeth also changed to cope with new feeding requirements.

SPEEDY AND STRONG
The wild tarpans of eastern Europe and western Asia, once famed for their strength and fast galloping, became extinct in the late19th century due to human interference. They were hunted for food, and their habitat became restricted. However, since they interbred, some horses of today show a number of their characteristics.

20

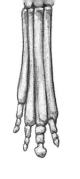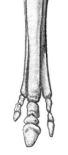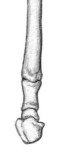

| Hyracotherium | Mesohippus | Merychippus | Pliohippus | Equus |

OVER MILLIONS OF YEARS

The four toes of *Hyracotherium* (HEYE-RA-COH-<u>THEER</u>-EE-UM) became three in *Mesohippus* (MEEZ-OH-<u>HIP</u>-US), side toes and a hoof in *Merychippus* (ME-REE-<u>KIP</u>-US), a hoof in *Pliohippus* (<u>PLEE</u>-OH-<u>HIP</u>-US), and then the hoof of the modern horse, *Equus* (<u>EK</u>-WUS.)

Once they would have fed on soft leaves. On the steppes, however, they turned to eating tough grasses and needed deeper, continuously growing teeth so that these did not ever wear down.

CAPTIVE SURVIVOR

Today, too, there is a horse on the verge of extinction, but we may yet be able to save it. Also known as the *takh* in the language of Mongolia, Przewalski's (PRZ-<u>VAL</u>-SKIS) horse stands just 53 inches tall at the shoulder and is the sole wild horse now existing. But it is found only in conservation areas and wildlife parks.

First discovered by a certain Colonel Przewalski in the late 19th century and named in his honor, its principal physical characteristics are an upright mane and a donkeylike tail with lengthier hairs at the bottom than at the top.

Long ago, in the wild they always lived in two types of group, each containing up to 20 individuals.

One was a family group of a male, perhaps two females, and their young. The other sort of group included only stallions.

Harsh weather was partly to blame for its decline. But it also interbred with domesticated ponies and was hunted by humans for its flesh and hide.

Several fossils of Przewalski's horse dating back thousands of years have been found. But one day perhaps captive stock will be returned to roam wild on the plains of Mongolia.

The Foundation for the Preservation and Protection of the Przewalski's horse has this as its aim.

CHANGE OF COAT

The coat of the tiny Przewalski's horse lightens to a pale yellow in the summer. In the winter, however, it darkens and thickens.

LOST WOLVES

Big, bad wolves are the stuff of folklore the world over, and their pelts have fetched high prices over the centuries. So perhaps it is not surprising that hunting has led to the extinction of some species.

DEEP IN THE HEART OF TEXAS
Hunting, interbreeding, and urban development caused the lamented Texas red wolf to disappear in the 1970s.

The handsome Newfoundland white wolf was given its scientific name, *Canis lupus beothucus* (<u>KAN</u>-IS <u>LOOP</u>-US <u>BEE</u>-OTH-<u>OO</u>-KUS), after the Beothuk Indians who once lived in this part of North America.

Weighing about 100 pounds and 6 feet in length, it had a most magnificent pure white pelt.

A HUNTED HUNTER
The Newfoundland white wolf was the first North American wolf to become extinct, in 1911. Those who shot one were rewarded by the government because they were considered a danger to local caribou.

But it is no more, like the group of Native American Indians after whom it was named; and a number of other wolves that once roamed various parts of the United States have also disappeared over the last century.

TEXAS TRAGEDY

Take the Texas red wolf, for example. This long-legged, lightweight species started to interbreed with black wolves and coyotes to produce a hybrid wolf population, and so the pure Texas red wolf went into decline. Its natural habitat also became destroyed over the years due to human settlement.

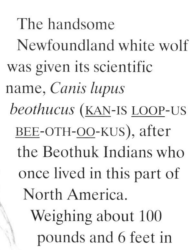

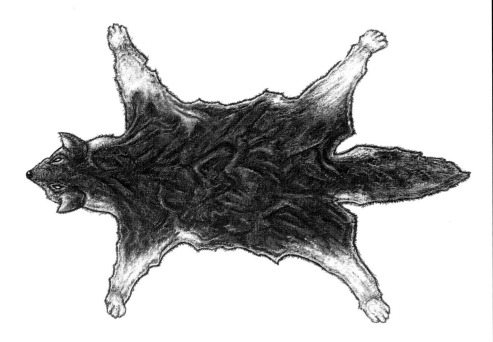

Other extinct North American wolves include the large Kenai wolf of Alaska, which hunted the huge moose of that region until its disappearance in 1915. The Great Plains Lobo wolf then went missing from a huge area between southern Manitoba and Saskatchewan in Canada down to Texas in 1926. The buff-colored Southern Rocky Mountain wolf of Colorado, Nevada, and Utah has not been seen since 1940; and the Cascade Mountain species, known as the brown wolf, is no longer to be found in British Columbia or Washington state.

A HIGH PRICE
The skin *above* is from the Japanese wolf. Its pelt was greatly valued, but at the start of the 20th century the world paid the ultimate price – its extinction.

WHAT A HOWLER!
In Japan a wolf known as the shamanu disappeared about 100 years ago. It was the smallest wolf ever known, but greatly feared because of its constant howling. In spite of this, it was hunted for its skin and also for its meat, which was favored by European visitors. Finally, the shamanu, or Japanese wolf, was driven to extinction by 1905.

Fact file

- Poisoned traps were once widely set for wolves, but these also caused the death of other creatures and, in turn, humans eating their meat.

- Some wolves were once even inoculated with a type of mange in order to destroy them; but the outcome was disastrous since the disease spread to cattle.

- The Florida black wolf became extinct in 1917. It was formerly found not only in Florida but in Tennessee and Alabama, too.

- The maned wolf is extinct in some parts of South America and currently endangered in Brazil and Paraguay.

- Few wolves are found now in Europe, but some still survive in remote parts of Italy, Spain, Greece, and Turkey.

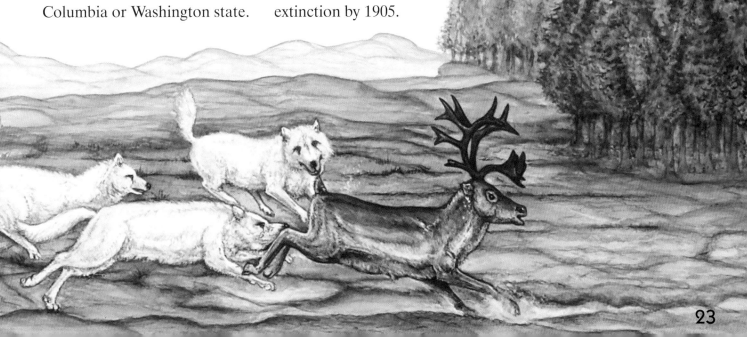

KOUPREY

A beast so rare that some once believed it had never existed at all and was merely mythical, or was long extinct, the kouprey first started to interest scientists when a few sightings were claimed during the 1930s. Since then, however, it has remained elusive.

A live kouprey is said to have been seen for the first time in living memory about 70 years ago, even though this creature had often been depicted in Cambodian temple carvings dating from as far back as the 11th century.

René Sauvel, a vet who was working in Cambodia for the French government, succeeded in capturing a young bull kouprey, and it was sent to the zoo at Vincennes, near Paris, France, where it was put on display. Another bull, an adult, was also taken at the time so that its anatomy could be studied.

It was then given the scientific name *Bos sauveli* (BOHS SO-<u>VAY</u>-LEE) in honor of Sauvel. The kouprey was rare even then and has only occasionally been spotted in more recent times. In fact, no one is certain if it still survives.

EXTINCT OR ELUSIVE?
No recent sightings of the kouprey, *right*, in its remote Far Eastern habitat have been confirmed.

The name kouprey comes from two Cambodian words – *kou*, meaning "cow," and *prey*, which translates as "forest."

How, though, did this creature evolve? Some researchers think that the kouprey could be a hybrid, the result of interbreeding. But some wildlife experts maintain it probably was, or maybe still is, an ancestor of Brahman cattle that became domesticated by farmers living in this part of the world.

So how does it differ in appearance from these cattle? It is said to stand about 6 feet tall and has a lengthy dewlap hanging from its throat and only a very slight ridge along its back, while this ridge is more pronounced in other Asian oxen. Its horns are also longer and more slender. A male kouprey's coat is gray-black, but it has white limbs.

The female, meanwhile, is a duller gray-brown in color. The species is definitely one of the world's rarest mammals.

Local hunters may well have been tempted to kill it for food, or over the years it may have become a victim of disease. In any event, it would be very difficult to locate one even if it has somehow managed to survive. Due to their coloring they are very hard to spot among the natural vegetation of the very dense Cambodian forests.

UNLUCKY ATTEMPTS

During the 1960s an attempt was made to find further specimens. However, at the time the area was a war zone, and the idea was dropped. During the 1980s what seemed to be a small herd was spotted at the border with Thailand, but an attempt to capture some of them was cut short when a landmine exploded.

In 1998 the Cambodian wildlife protection authorities made an attempt to trace the creature, and a claim was made that another herd had been sighted near the Vietnamese border, but there is no conclusive evidence of this. However, if a live kouprey *is* finally captured, scientists will be able to test its DNA and prove whether or not it has a different genetic makeup from other oxen.

Fact file

- Some koupreys are thought to have existed not only in Cambodia but in Laos, Vietnam, and Thailand, too.

- In 1964 the kouprey was still to be found in large numbers in Cambodia and was even chosen as that country's national animal in that year. However, due to warfare in the region and to overhunting it went into rapid decline.

- Whether the kouprey was always a feral (wild) creature or whether it was domesticated at some time, no one is sure.

- A scientist at Harvard University, Dr. H.J. Coolidge, became so convinced the kouprey was a completely new species that he suggested it should have a special name – *Novibos,* or "new ox."

Bounty-hunters, meanwhile, with no respect for the survival of this creature, have offered several thousand dollars for a pair of kouprey horns.

MAIN FEATURES
The portrait of a kouprey in profile, *below,* shows its principal characteristics – white legs, gray-black body, curved horns, dewlap, and low-ridged back.

CHALICOTHERIUM

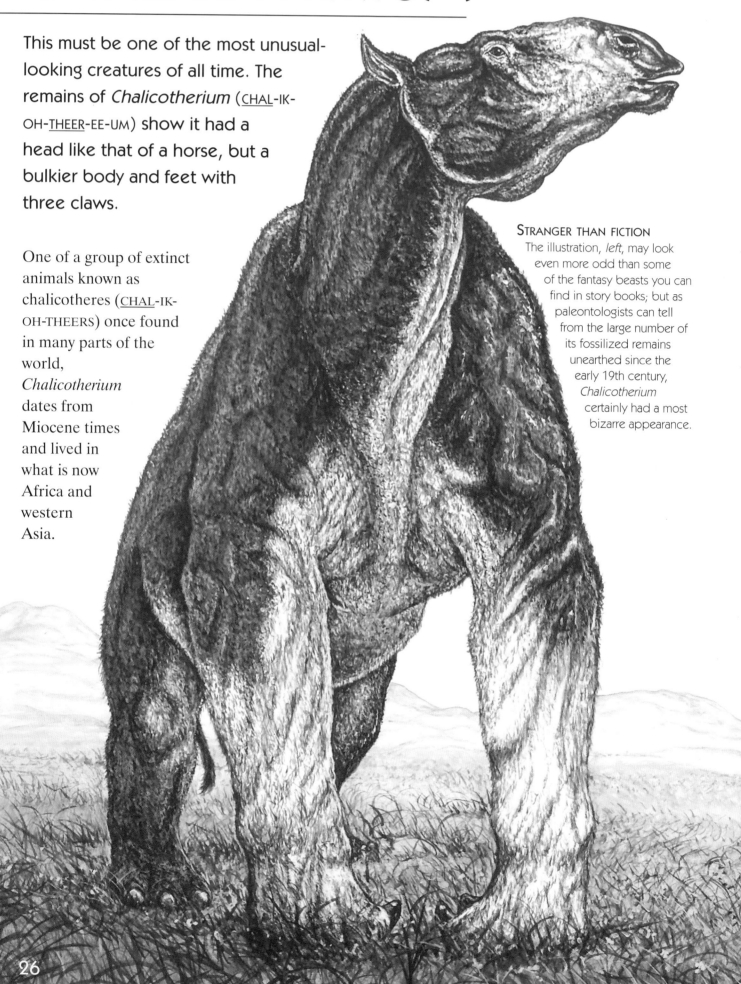

This must be one of the most unusual-looking creatures of all time. The remains of *Chalicotherium* (CHAL-IK-OH-THEER-EE-UM) show it had a head like that of a horse, but a bulkier body and feet with three claws.

One of a group of extinct animals known as chalicotheres (CHAL-IK-OH-THEERS) once found in many parts of the world, *Chalicotherium* dates from Miocene times and lived in what is now Africa and western Asia.

STRANGER THAN FICTION
The illustration, *left*, may look even more odd than some of the fantasy beasts you can find in story books; but as paleontologists can tell from the large number of its fossilized remains unearthed since the early 19th century, *Chalicotherium* certainly had a most bizarre appearance.

NEW EVIDENCE

The first complete skeleton of a chalicothere was found by the French paleontologist Henri Filhol in 1887. Until then only a few teeth, portions of skulls, and claws belonging to different specimens had been unearthed, and they had led to some confusion. Claws discovered in 1823 were even thought to have been from some sort of nonexistent giant pangolin at first, according to another esteemed French paleontologist, Georges Cuvier, who was usually more reliable in his conclusions.

The teeth discovered had clearly belonged to an ungulate (a hoofed herbivore such as a horse, a deer, or an elephant). So Cuvier thought that the fossilized claws must have been from another animal entirely. Only when a whole fossilized skeleton came to light was Cuvier proved wrong. It was possible after all for an animal with an ungulate's teeth to have clawed feet.

The chalicotheres survived for about 25 million years in all, but not many of their fossils have been found, indicating they did not live in herds.

Other chalicotheres, relatives of *Chalicotherium*, include *Moropus* (MOOR-OHP-US), with a name meaning "sloth foot" given because of its slow movement and claws. It stood about 8 feet in height and also had far longer forelimbs than its back legs. However, it preferred to stand on its stout rear limbs to feed from the soft leaves of trees rather than bending down to eat grass, which it would have found difficult to digest.

Some paleontologists have suggested that *Moropus* may even have had a long, prehensile tongue just as some perissodactyls (*see* Fact file box on this page) do today. However, we cannot be sure it had this sort of grasping tongue since no soft tissue ever becomes fossilized, as bones do. But such a tongue would certainly have helped it get hold of vegetation while feeding.

As a rule, *Moropus* held its head high, as *Chalicotherium* did. But a special ball-and-socket joint in their skeletal structure also enabled both these chalicotheres to reach down to the ground to drink.

Fact file

- *Chalicotherium* remains have been unearthed in Africa and in Europe. The fossilized bones of related chalicotheres, meanwhile, have been dug up in North America and Asia.

- Using its foot claws, *Chalicotherium* – a herbivore – would have been able to dig up roots on which to feed.

- It probably also reared up on its two hind legs or sat on its haunches to feed directly from high bushes and trees.

- Chalicotheres were mammals and also perissodactyls – creatures with an odd number of toes.

- From its skeletal remains paleontologists agree that *Chalicotherium* must have looked like a cross between a horse, a giraffe, and a gorilla.

Other chalicotheres included *Phylotillon* (FEYE-LOT-IL-ON) and *Macrotherium* (MAC-ROH-THEER-EE-UM). All of them were large and strong creatures, but the entire family finally became extinct during the last Ice Age, about 12,000 years ago. Precisely why remains a complete mystery.

LOST ASSES

Middle-Eastern carvings dating back to 650 B.C. show the Syrian wild ass being caught. It was mainly the young, however, that were killed for their meat. The last of these animals died in the wild in 1927. Since then other asses have become endangered, too.

Also known as the Syrian onager, this ass, shown *below*, inhabited a far wider area than just Syria in spite of its name and once lived in Palestine, Arabia, Iraq, and beyond. Here, for at least two thousand years it was hunted by humans but often managed to survive due to the tremendous speed with which it could escape from human predators.

The onager was hunted in various ways. Sometimes it would be lassoed; but it would also be run down by dogs, shot with bows and arrows, or tripped up by metal spikes. Worse was to come. Once guns and vehicles reached the Middle East, the Syrian onager became more vulnerable. Eventually, the hunting of it reached a peak during World War I (1914-1918.) According to Islamic dietary laws, the meat of the onager could be eaten because it was not considered a domestic animal. However, a number of Bedhouin kept them.

ON DIET

The Syrian wild ass or onager was small, only measuring about 3 feet in height at the most. It was very lightweight, too, perhaps because, as a herbivore, it would not have found much grazing land or suitable food in a desert environment. Indeed, it may sometimes have killed and been tempted to eat the occasional tiny mammal, such as the mouse in this illustration.

A few young ones were often to be found tethered in the these nomads' tents in preparation for slaughter at a feast because their meat was considered a delicacy.

In spite of this, it is possible that the onager, if not shot or killed for its flesh, lived to a ripe old age. Some Arabic texts even mention that they sometimes reached the age of two hundred! However, this wording is likely to have been an exaggerated generalization in an attempt to make it clear that onagers were hardy.

THIRSTY ANIMALS
The Syrian wild ass could live for only two or three days without drinking and was therefore usually found close to water sources.

DYING BREEDS

Today there are other types of asses that are have become severely endangered. One is the Asiatic wild ass from Mongolia. Also known as the *kulan*, it is very fleet of foot and is said to run as fast as 40 miles per hour! Its hide and meat have long been highly prized, but herds are protected by law now.

The so-called Persian wild ass, meanwhile, is smaller than other Asiatic wild asses and now found only in a small area of Iran, as well as part of Russia, where a reserve was established for it. Severe winters, however, took their toll; and the few taken there failed to reproduce at first. Later, though, several replacements were bred far more successfully.

NOW AND FOREVER?
The photograph *right* shows a wild ass of today. With the help of carefully planned conservation programs and reserves we should be able to save them for posterity.

The Persian wild ass was once also sometimes found in Afghanistan, but has not been seen there for very many years and is presumed extinct. The Indian and Tibetan species of wild ass, known as the *kiang,* meanwhile are also in severe decline.

One of two types of African onagers, the Somali is tall, reaching 4 feet in height, and found in Ethiopia, Eritrea, and northern Somalia.

But constant wars and political upheavals there have made sightings of these creatures increasingly scarce. Only a few hundred are thought to exist, while in Somalia alone there were were once at least 10,000. In Somalia, too, they have been hunted for their fat, which some of the population once believed would protect them against tuberculosis.

The Nubian ass, the other African species, is also rare and found only in a small part of Sudan and Eritrea. However, no one is entirely sure whether these surviving creatures are

Fact file

- The scientific name for the Syrian wild ass is *Equus hemionus hemippus* (<u>EK</u>-WOOS HEM-EE-<u>OHN</u>-US HEM-<u>IP</u>-US.)

- Hunting of the Syrian wild ass dates back over 2,500 years, as evidenced by scenes depicted on ancient carvings.

- Before horses were brought to the Middle East about 4,000 years ago, the onager was harnessed and used as a draft animal for pulling carts and chariots.

- There are references to the wild ass in both the Old Testament and the Koran.

- The last wild Syrian ass was shot in 1927 when it came to drink at an oasis.

- Onagers lived and fed in small family groups.

truly the original wild species. They might well be domesticated asses that have somehow managed to escape from captivity, or that have been released by their owners into remote regions.

RAT-RABBIT

Chances are you find the thought of eating rat flesh absolutely disgusting. But the so-called rat-rabbit, also known as the pika and eaten in prehistoric times when game was scarce, was actually a lagomorph, as rabbits and hares are, and not a rodent.

If you look in a traditional French cookbook, you will find lots of recipes for dishes that include rabbit or hare meat. So it is hardly surprising that way back in time, inhabitants of the French island of Corsica hunted the local pikas, or rat-rabbits.

Also known as mouse-hares or coneys, these creatures actually looked more like a cross between rabbits and guinea pigs.

No one can be sure today, but their roasted flesh probably tasted a little like chicken, but with a stronger flavor.

To judge from the many fossilized bones paleontologists have found, the Corsican pika must have been very common during the last Ice Age and is thought to have disappeared from this part of the world in about 500 A.D. However, until the 18th century there was another related Mediterranean pika on the island of Sardinia.

The last record of the Sardinian rat-rabbit dates from 1774, when a traveler wrote that huge numbers of their burrows were to be found all over the island. There is no evidence of them after that, however, so we can only assume that this species, too, was eradicated by predators.

According to one theory, the pikas, or rat-rabbits, originally crossed from the mainland of what is now Europe at a time when there were land bridges to the islands of Corsica and Sardinia. They were forced to remain there, however, after the sea levels rose, and there was no return route for them.

ON THE ICE-AGE MENU
When larger prey was in short supply, nothing would have been more welcome than a few rat-rabbits to roast for a prehistoric supper.

INTOLERANT OVER TERRITORY
If extinct pikas behaved like one of today, shown *above*, they were fiercely territorial, fighting with others over what they regarded as their own space.

Some of these extinct rat-rabbits are thought to have grown to more than 12 inches in length. They probably moved quickly, but their human predators used spears and also set traps to catch them.

As for other aspects of the Corsican pika's appearance and behavior, we have to look to those pikas that exist in other parts of the world today. Those of North America, for example, are principally rock-dwellers. Very intolerant of each other, they live a solitary existence most of the time. They do not hibernate but collect vegetation during the summer as a food source for the winter months, during which they also continue to forage for meals.

Strangely, pikas of today produce green droppings during the day, but black droppings at night. They also eat their own waste at times to retain nutrients. It is possible extinct rat-rabbits did this, too.

ZAGLOSSUS

Spiny anteaters use their long, slender snouts to sniff out their staple diet – the insects forming part of their name. Scenes like this take place regularly in remote parts of Australia and southern New Guinea where they live. But long ago there was a *giant* spiny anteater, more than twice the size of those existing today.

BIG AND BRISTLY

Who would have imagined that a spiny anteater the size of a sheep once existed! It was the largest of this type of creature ever known.

Known to paleontologists as *Zaglossus hacketti* (ZAG-<u>LOSS</u>-US HAK-<u>ET</u>-EE), this ancient spiny anteater (or echidna) existed on Earth at a time when dinosaurs were still roaming the planet. Like today's echidna, which it resembled closely, it would have had a very long and sticky tongue that was ideal for lapping up meals of ants and termites.

The coat of this ancient ant-eater consisted of numerous coarse hairs and spines that provided at least some degree of protection against enemies and might also have camouflaged the creature well. Nevertheless, it would frequently have fallen victim to any of the large predators with which it coexisted long ago.

Zagolossus hacketti was also what scientists call a monotreme. (This word means "single hole" and refers to the urinary, digestive, and reproductive organs that have a single opening.)

The echidna of today is also a monotreme and so, by the way, is the duck-billed platypus. But *Zaglossus hacketti*, as we can tell from remains, was about twice the size of the modern 20-inch-long echidna.

Monotremes are most unusual creatures for another reason, too. Although strictly speaking they are mammals since they provide milk for their young, they lay eggs rather than giving birth to live offspring. Indeed, today's echnidna will lay a single egg that hatches into a pouch.

LARGE APPETITE
Zaglossus hacketti probably fed in exactly the same way as an echidna of today, as shown in the photograph *above,* but would have eaten far more.

We can only assume that the prehistoric *Zaglossus* did the same; and like today's baby monotremes, the young may also have obtained nourishment by licking at the milk that its mother excreted directly into the pouch.

The prehistoric *Zaglossus* is also likely to have been a nocturnal animal, living primarily in arid, desertlike regions. During the day it would have slept, venturing out when the temperature was cooler. But today a short-beaked species is found not only in deserts but in forests and meadows. A long-beaked species, meanwhile, is only found in a mountainous zone of New Guinea.

Modern spiny anteaters have long been regarded as stupid creatures. Recently, however, debate has arisen because they have been found to have surprisingly large brains for their size.

Fact file

- Today's echidna, or spiny anteater, is a shy creature and uses its strong claws to dig into the ground and hide if danger threatens.

- Although *Zaglossus hacketti* was large, it may well have gone underground, too, until the coast was clear.

- *Zaglossus* was part of Australia's so-called megafauna (large creatures.)

- No one knows for sure whether the Aborigines of Australia, who settled there at least 60,000 years ago, were responsible in any way for the disappearance of this giant species of anteater.

- Today there are two smaller species of echidnas that survive in Australia, Tasmania, and New Guinea.

It seems likely that a spiny anteater the size of prehistoric *Zaglossus hacketti* may well have had an even bigger brain than the echidnas of today and so would have been quite intelligent.

For some time a scientist called Peggy Rismiller has been studying the wildlife on Kangaroo Island, near Adelaide, a main city in southern Australia. She has a particular interest in the echidna population that survives there and as a result of her research may well come up with a few more clues as to the life of their ancient relatives, of which *Zaglossus hacketti* was by far the largest.

THYLACINE

At the end of the 19th century farmers offered payment for every single thylacine killed since they believed them to be a threat to their livestock. Now, however, following total extinction of this highly unusual marsupial, scientists are enthusiastic about possibly being able to bring them back to life.

TAKE THAT TIGER!
In 1886 a government-supported campaign to kill as many thylacines as possible was started. As a result, thousands of these creatures died at the hands of bounty-hunters, and the pelts were sold to fur-dealers for considerable profit.

ON HIS GUARD
The photographer who took this rare shot of a live thylacine dared not venture closer for fear of being attacked.

Thousands of years ago these nocturnal hunters inhabited much of Australia, fossil evidence shows; but in more recent times they seem to have lived only on the island of Tasmania, south of the main continent. Extending to about 5 feet in length, including a long, rigid tail, the thylacine closely resembled a wolf.

But there was one main difference – there were dark brown or black stripes that ran across the thylacine's back and hind quarters. This was in fact how the thylacine also became known by two other names – the Tasmanian tiger or the Tasmanian wolf. However, though like wolves and tigers, it was a rather special type of mammal – a marsupial.

PRESERVED FOR POSTERITY?
One day it may be possible to produce live specimens of extinct thylacines by using genetic material from one that died at birth and that has been preserved.

Just like the marsupials of today – kangaroos and wallabies, for instance – it had a pouch within which its young would be carried shortly after birth.

On the island of Tasmania thylacines were frequently blamed for killing sheep until finally the government agreed that anyone who shot a thylacine could be rewarded. This offer naturally attracted hundreds of bounty-hunters, so that sometimes several would be shot by a single gunman in one day.

However, thylacines were not always responsible for the death of sheep and so were sometimes shot for no real reason. There was also a brisk trade in thylacine skins, so that by 1910 very few of these creatures were left in the wild. Finally, when the Australian authorities announced that the thylacine was an endangered species and should be protected by law, it was too late.

There was only one specimen left in the zoo in Hobart, Tasmania's capital, so it could not be bred. Benjamin – the last of the thylacines – died there in captivity on September 7, 1936. Scientists may have some surprises in store, however.

POSSIBLE REVIVAL?

Researchers at the Australian Museum in Sydney have been studying DNA taken from a thylacine baby that had been preserved in a jar of alcohol after its death in 1866.

Because this genetic material is of such high quality, they think they may be able to clone the creature by inserting the DNA into the empty egg of a similar species. This species might then give birth to a thylacine.

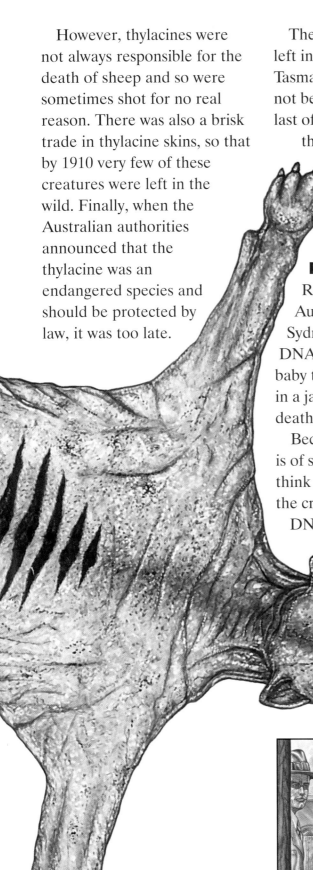

Fact file

- The thylacine was a marsupial and had a backward-opening pouch much like that of the opossums we know today.

- Well over 1,000 years ago, when it was native to Australia, the thylacine fed on kangaroos and wallabies.

- A thylacine was so fierce, even a whole pack of dogs would be terrified by the sight of one. However, they rarely attacked humans and only hunted singly after dark.

- Many thylacines died when, in 1910, they fell victim to a disease like distemper.

- Thylacines could rear up on their hind legs in a threatening position.

- Female thylacines usually had four babies at a time, which they carried in their pouch.

It is something the museum's director, Professor Michael Archer, believes they could achieve within 10 years; but the estimated cost – more than $40 million – may be totally prohibitive.

MAIN ATTRACTION
The thylacine shown *right* was for many years a very popular animal at Tasmania's Hobart Zoo. But it had no mate and must have disliked being caged and stared at.

DEINOGALERIX

Paleontologists have discovered in southern Italy what looks like a type of extinct hedgehog in rocks dating back 25 million years to Miocene times. But unlike the hedgehogs we know today, this species seems to have been extraordinarily large and to have had a tail.

A THORNY PROBLEM
The modern hedgehog *above* is becoming increasingly endangered. Many are run over, shot by gamekeepers, or killed by foxes.

Creatures resembling hedgehogs are thought to have lived as far back as 80 million years ago in Cretaceous times, when dinosaurs such as *Triceratops* and *Tyrannosaurus rex* roamed parts of our planet. But it is possible that large *Deinogalerix* (<u>DEYE</u>-NO-<u>GAL</u>-ER-IKS) did not evolve as a species until much later.

Its fossilized remains, first discovered in 1973, show it was several times the size of a modern hedgehog. Other characteristics included a long, slim face; small, pointed ears; a lengthy, tapering tail; and of course, its long hairs. Scientists believe it was an insectivore, feeding on beetles, dragonflies, and crickets mainly; but it may also have hunted snails, small mammals, reptiles, and birds.

Long ago what is now Italy was a group of small islands. Only later did most join with mainland Europe. A known feature of island life is that creatures isolated there sometimes grow to a different size from those found elsewhere, which may explain why *Deinogalerix* was about five times the size of a hedgehog of today. But of course, no one can be sure whether its remains may one day be found elsewhere, thereby entirely disproving such a theory.

Today's hedgehogs roll up into a ball as a form of camouflage if they are frightened. But no one knows either whether prehistoric *Deinogalerix* protected itself in this way. Perhaps since it was the size of a small dog, it had no need to do this.

It is not known for certain why *Deinogalerix* died out, but scientists have suggested it may not have been able to find sufficient food for its needs, or maybe all were lost in some form of natural disaster. Whatever the case, its demise cannot, at least for the moment, be reversed. What though, can we do to preserve the hedgehog of *today*? Some plan of action is definitely needed since its numbers are decreasing with every passing year in some parts of the world. It is a sad loss because they are in fact ideal natural pest-controllers.

Some get stabbed by accident with garden implements when they are sleeping in compost heaps, so it is important to use these tools gently. Others die through eating insects that have been poisoned by pesticides. They may eat hundreds of such bugs in the course of a week and build up dangerous residues. Even if they do not die at once, when hibernating they use up contaminated body fat and are likely to perish.

The hedgehog of today has few enemies. Badgers eat them; but if we are not careful, they may finally be destroyed due to human negligence.

Fact file

- The name *Deinogalerix* has the meaning "terrible hedgehog." But no one knows if it was fiercer than the gentle hedgehogs of today.

- *Deinogalerix* was probably a solitary creature, like the hedgehog of today, and did not live in groups.

- Modern male hedgehogs sometimes fight with each other, particularly in the spring when they are looking for mates. *Deinogalerix* may well have behaved in a similar way.

- Like the baby hedgehogs of today, *Deinogalerix* may have been born without spines; but they probably appeared not long after birth. It is likely they were soft and white at first, only later hardening and changing color.

AWAKE IN WINTER?
Hedgehogs of today hibernate in winter. But scientists remain uncertain as to whether the prehistoric hedgehoglike creature known as *Deinogalerix* found this necessary.

LOST WALLABIES

Wallabies are among the most endearing of all Australia's marsupials. Sadly, however, a few species were hunted to extinction by human predators who took their pelts and cooked their meat. Foxes have also contributed to their disappearance.

CUTE BUT KILLED
Grey's wallabies, *below*, were stalked at night by foxes, when they were less wary of being caught. In spite of being fleet of foot, they were often overrun and taken for meals of raw flesh.

The main characteristic of a Grey's wallaby was its lengthy tail. It was almost as long as the rest of its body. Reputedly very fast on its feet, it would often wait until the very last moment before bounding away at a tremendous rate to avoid being caught.

RISKY TACTICS

This must undoubtedly have contributed to the demise of Grey's wallabies. Time was clearly of the essence even for such a speedy creature as Grey's wallaby if it was to remain alive.

Another factor that almost certainly had a part to play in the road to extinction was its preference for open ground as a habitat. This meant there was rarely anywhere for it to hide when threatened.

Another type of wallaby – the white-throated species – was once also thought to have died out in 1932 in a region of New South Wales, Australia, where it was once plentiful. Destruction of its natural habitat was to blame. But perhaps we are sometimes too rash in declaring an animal extinct because in 1966, entirely unexpectedly, this wallaby suddenly reappeared across the water in New Zealand.

YOUNG VICTIMS
The babies of Grey's wallabies were frequently attacked even though protected in the mother's pouch, just as the "joey" of another species of wallaby is *above*.

LOST AND FOUND

Experts were stumped at first. How could Grey's wallaby possibly have reached those shores? Then it was discovered that a number of these wallabies had in fact been introduced to New Zealand by settlers at the end of the 19th century, remaining undisturbed there in the wild.

CATCH ME IF YOU CAN!
The extinct hare-wallaby, *right*, would sometimes not run off until the last moment when being chased by a hunting dog, as if issuing a challenge.

Amazingly, too, a small number were rediscovered in a remote area back in Australia in 1972.

Another member of this family that seems no longer to be with us is the Eastern hare-wallaby. It had the scientific name *Lagorchestes leporides* (LARG-OR-KEST-EEZ LEP-OR-EE-DEEZ,) and there were several species in this family. It was given its common name because of its close resemblance to the European hare. Sometimes it was shot purely for sport; but it was also taken for its meat and skin, and foxes went in for the kill, too.

Some types of wallabies are still found in large numbers. Others of these kangaroolike creatures, however, are declining, among them the ring-tailed rock wallaby, the bridled nail-tailed wallaby, and the crescent nail-tailed species, all of which feature on the danger lists of particular Australian states.

39

BARBARY LION

Fierce man-eaters and weighing 500 pounds or more when fully grown, Barbary lions were finally doomed to become extinct in the wild due to the activity of lion-hunting tribes and the rise of banditry in the mountains of Morocco, northern Africa.

Known by the scientific name *Panthera leo leo* (PAN-THERR-A LEE-OH LEE-OH), Barbary lions once lived exclusively in the woodlands of the Atlas Mountains of North Africa and were separated geographically from the other lion populations of that continent by this range.

Extremely muscular and with thick manes extending over half their upper bodies and the belly when mature, these lions were a darker shade than others of their continent.

MIGHTY MAN-EATER
The Barbary lion was a close relation of the lions we know today but far larger. Its massive mane was a very impressive feature.

40

SYMBOLS OF POWER

Today they are no longer found in the wild. But four hundred of these fierce beasts were once kept by the Roman Emperor Julius Caesar, while his great rival Pompey is thought to have owned as many as six hundred.

In Libya the last Barbary lion was killed at the very end of the 17th century. About 160 years later there is a record of one being paraded through the streets of Algiers, capital city of Algeria. But the government of that time encouraged Algerian tribes who hunted the Barbary lion to kill as many as possible and offered a high price for their skins. Those who killed these creatures were also excused from paying taxes. The former 20th-century ruler of Abyssinia (now Ethiopia), Haile Salassie, also kept a few Barbary lions.

ACCORDING TO ANCIENT LEGEND
The story goes that Androcles, right, was rewarded for removing a thorn from a Barbary lion's paw. The lion recalled this act and later spared his life in the arena.

BARBARY BREEDING
The photograph left shows the baby Barbary lion, Saffi, bred at a British zoo. If such experiments continue, this species of lion may one day be released back into the wild.

They were safely tethered in his throne room as a symbol of his power, and some are still found in captivity in Morocco.

STAGING A COMEBACK

In an attempt to provide a genetic match to the Barbary lions used by the Romans, British researcher Kay Hill – founder of the conservation charity Wildlink International – has been granted permission to take bone samples from the dungeons under Rome's Colosseum.

Meanwhile, at Port Lympne Zoo in Kent, England, two lions descended from those still owned by the Moroccan royal family mated. The result was a she-cub, Saffi, born at the zoo in July 1999.

These three lions, scientists hope, together with two others born the following year, will

provide a starting point for breeding the Barbary lion back to existence. Perhaps in the future they will be placed in safari parks in their former North African natural habitat.

LOST BANDICOOTS

Although some bandicoots survive, several species of this cute-looking, tiny marsupial became extinct during the 20th century. The fur trade was partly to blame, but so was loss of their natural habitat. They were also widely preyed on by foxes.

Discovered in 1840 but virtually extinct just 100 years later in the Australian states of Victoria and New South Wales, the eastern barred bandicoot can nevertheless still be found in small numbers on the island of Tasmania. Some of the difficulties it faces there are almost certainly similar to those its extinct cousins from the mainland must have come up against, including predation by foxes and dogs, as well as a disease caught from cats.

BURNED TO DEATH
The eastern barred bandicoot did not burrow and so was killed only too readily in the face of fire.

Today in Tasmania the clearing of grasslands for agricultural use is leading to further decline in the eastern barred bandicoots' numbers, too, even though they reproduce numerously. A single female may give birth to as many as 16 offspring in just one year.

They are known to have a strong sense of smell and use it before digging in the soil with their claws for food such as grubs, worms, beetles, and roots. Berries also form an important part of their diet.

They are solitary animals and only get together with others of their species when breeding.

The western barred bandicoot has also disappeared from mainland Australia and was last recorded there in 1922. It had a single stripe at its sides, just by its thighs, a backward-opening pouch, and weighed only about 7 ounces on average. It was not seen for a great many years, but was rediscovered in 1983 on the two little-known nearby islands of Bernier and Dorre.

Here, they live mainly in sandhills behind beaches or in dunes and come out only at night to feed on vegetation and insects. The population of these western bandicoots remains fairly stable on the two islands for the moment because conditions have hardly changed there over the centuries.

But if large numbers of foxes, sheep, goats, cats, or rabbits are ever introduced, the situation would almost certainly be different, and the western bandicoot could well become lost forever.

A BARRED BANDICOOT
The eastern barred bandicoot, *above*, is recognizable by the few stripes on its rump. The western species, however, can be distinguished by a single bar.

The pig-footed bandicoot, meanwhile, was given its name because its front limbs closely resembled pigs' trotters. It once lived in South Australia but seems to have died out in 1907, although claims have been made that it was spotted in 1925. Since then, however, no one has caught sight of this orange-brown bandicoot. But Australian Aborigines have recorded that the pig-footed bandicoot liked to feast on termites and ants, and that it could run at tremendous speed.

Bilbies, also known as rabbit-bandicoots, were once to be found in South Australia, too, but have now entirely disappeared from this state. Early settlers found them delightful and tried to protect these bandicoots. But in time people began to lose interest, and economics gradually took over, so that these small creatures were increasingly killed for their pelts. Some also perished when they became caught in rabbit traps or were killed by poisoned bait meant for dingoes.

There were in fact two types of bilbie – the greater, with silky, blue-gray fur, and the lesser, which was smaller and duller in color. Especially cute as they slept, they did not lie down but squatted, folding their ears over their eyes and tucking their muzzles between their front limbs.

Fact file

- The eastern barred bandicoot is endangered in the wild and only found in Tasmania.

- The habitat of the western barred bandicoot once included woodlands, shrubland, and heathlands. Its decline in such terrain was probably due to the introduction of foxes, rabbits, and other predatory animals.

- The western barred bandicoot was nocturnal and spent its day asleep in its nest.

- Bandicoots belong to a family with the scientific name *Peramelidae* (PE-RAM-<u>EL</u>-ID-EYE.)

- The largest known species of bandicoot was the greater rabbit-bandicoot, which had a 10-inch-long tail. It lived in South Australia and became extinct in 1930.

GIANT BEAVER

Modern beavers are very much like their distant cousins, the giant beavers that died out about 10,000 years ago. But there were several differences, the main one being size. Where, then, did the giant beaver live? And what can be learned from the many legends associated with this prehistoric creature?

One of the largest rodents ever to exist on Earth, giant beavers are known to have lived alongside such creatures as the woolly mammoth and the saber-toothed tiger in what is now North America. However, although Stone Age humans left memorials to a number of prehistoric creatures in their cave paintings, no depictions have ever been discovered of the giant beaver. Scientists have therefore had to rely on skeletal remains and Native American folk tales for information as to what this awesome creature must have looked like.

UNDERNEATH IT ALL
The reconstructed skeleton *right* is of a type of giant beaver known as *Palaeocastor* (PAL-EE-OH-KAS-TOR.). Its remains were found in Nebraska. Note the long and broad front feet. It did not build dams, as modern beavers do, but dug spiraling tunnels to underground homes.

PETRIFYING BEAST

According to the oral tradition of an Indian tribe, there was once a large lake, home to a particularly fierce beaver, in the Connecticut River valley. Sometimes the beast became so hungry that it would come ashore, run amok, and attack humans. Naturally, the local population was terrified by this possibility. They therefore called on a spirit called Hobomock and asked him to kill the creature.

Legend has it that he cut off its head with a mighty stake. The giant beaver then sank to the depths of the lake, where it turned to stone, just like its fossilized remains.

Indian belief even has it that evidence of the existence of this huge creature lies in certain features of the landscape. Look to Mount Sugar Loaf, they say, if you want to see the remains of the upturned head of the beaver and to a northward range for its body. The hollow that lies between these two areas is said to be where Hobomock struck the creature's neck and severed its skull.

The first recorded remains of a giant beaver were unearthed in 1837 in Ohio. But since then several complete specimens and bones have been found in many parts of North America – everywhere, in fact, from Florida to the Yukon and from the central states to New York.

AS BIG AS A BEAR

The giant beaver skeleton on display in Chicago's Field Museum is 8 feet long. When fleshed out, it would have weighed six times as much as a modern beaver.

Not only were giant beavers of the past much larger in build than beavers of today, their teeth were also entirely different. Indeed, their cutting teeth were up to 6 inches long, and their cheek teeth were much bigger than those of modern beavers, too.

There is fossil evidence that some lived north of the Arctic Circle in the Yukon, one set of bones dating back 130,000 years. As lakes appeared when it became warmer and ice sheets melted between periods of glaciation, they may have swum north.

NOW KILLED FOR COATS

Giant beavers lived alongside early human beings for thousands of years, yet there is no evidence that they were hunted for their pelts or for food. Today, however, modern beavers like the one shown *right* could become endangered because they are sometimes killed for the fashion industry.

CURIOUS STRUCTURES

Scientists have also found the remains of the homes of these prehistoric beavers. Dating from Miocene times, they were first discovered by prospectors looking for gold in the American Midwest who entirely by accident came across odd corkscrewlike shapes in the ground, extending to about seven feet in depth.

At first, these strange structures were thought by paleobotanists possibly to be the fossil casts of huge, ancient tree roots. Other scientists, however, suggested bolts of lightning had caused the spirals to form. Finally, however, the mystery was solved when it was realized they were in fact underground pathways to the homes of giant beavers.

Fact file

- The scientific name for the prehistoric American giant beaver is *Castoroides* (KAS-TOR-OY-DEEZ).

- European species of slightly smaller giant beavers also existed during the last Ice Age, and so there may be remains that date from 2 million years ago still to be dug up.

- Giant beaver fossils found in Toronto, Canada, are over 70,000 years old.

- The giant beaver was one of the largest rodents ever to have existed.

- What may once have been a giant beaver's home was found in Ohio in 1912. Close by the long, descending, spiral-shaped entrance, the skull of a giant beaver was also unearthed.

GLOSSARY

antipodean
living on the other side of the globe

camouflage
to disguise to avoid being seen

clone
to use genetic material for making an identical creature

conservation
care of flora and fauna

coprolites
fossilized dung

cyclops
a fabled one-eyed monster

dewlap
skin hanging under the throat of an ox

DNA
deoxyribonucelic (DEE-OX-EE-REYE-BOH NOO-KLAY-IK) acid, a substance responsible for passing on hereditary characteristics

domesticated
tamed and living alongside humans

habitat
the natural environment in which a creature lives

hybrid
the offspring of two different species

incisors
cutting teeth

insectivore
a creature that eats insects

mammal
any animal giving birth to live young and suckling them

marsupial
a creature carrying its young in a pouch

medieval
from the Middle Ages, a period of European history lasting from about 600 to 1400 A.D.

Mediterranean
part of southern Europe and also a sea in that region

Miocene times
a period of prehistoric time lasting from 24.5 to 5 million years ago

monotreme
an animal with a single opening for its reproductive and excreting organs

naturalist
someone with an interest in natural history

nocturnal
coming out by night

paleobotanist
a scientist who studies the fossils of plants and trees

paleontologist
a scientist who studies fossils

pelt
an animal's skin or fur

Pleistocene times
a period lasting from about 1 to 2 million years ago

predator
an animal that hunts another

prey
the victim of a predator

pygmy
a dwarf creature

reserve
a special area kept aside to provide a suitable environment for animals to roam free

stallion
a male horse

tusks
very elongated, protruding teeth, as in elephants

vampire
a fantasy creature said to come out at night and feed on blood

veld
open grassland in southern Africa

zoologist
a scientist who studies different types of animal life

46